# CIGARETTES AND ROCKET SHIPS

Scott Delaney

Cover Illustration by Amy Barrow.

Copyright 2019 by Scott Delaney. All Rights Reserved.
Published by Broken Column Press.
BrokenColumnPress.com
ISBN: 978-1-944616-16-8

**Thank You**

Mum, Dad, Bart, Blake
Ed
Kristine

# Table of Contents

Cast of Characters .................................................................. i

Forward ................................................................................. 1

    Pen to Paper ...................................................................... 3

Lost ....................................................................................... 5

    Lineage ............................................................................... 7

    Amongst the Waves ......................................................... 8

    Demigod Breath ................................................................ 9

    The Dopest of Dope ....................................................... 10

    Shipwrecked .................................................................... 11

    The Myth .......................................................................... 12

    Once .................................................................................. 13

    Sun Blister ........................................................................ 14

Lost-Found ......................................................................... 15

    Empty Mind ..................................................................... 17

    Warrior Fairy ................................................................... 18

    Get By ............................................................................... 19

    Picture Frames ................................................................ 20

    The Challenge .................................................................. 21

    Eire Assassin ................................................................... 22

    Tug ..................................................................................... 23

    Cigarettes and Rocket Ships ......................................... 24

    Here ................................................................................... 25

- Found ............................................................ 27
    - Nico ......................................................... 29
    - Whispers ................................................. 30
    - Tried ........................................................ 31
    - Leper Hugs (Truth of Nico) ................. 32
    - Editing Insight ...................................... 33
    - Fail Great ............................................... 34
    - Lilac Dreams ......................................... 35
    - Defined ................................................... 36
    - All I've Found ....................................... 37
    - Time Travelers ...................................... 38
- Epilogue ..................................................... 39
    - Truth ....................................................... 41

# Cast of Characters

**Lord Helios**
    Adventurer
**Amongst the Waves**
    Lord Helios' First Love
**Leukothea**
    Goddess of Wayward Travelers
**Zim**
    King Fairy, Lord Helios' Friend
**Ea**
    Eire Assassin, Lord Helios' Friend
**Kohol**
    Lord Helios' Toxic Love
**Nico**
    Lord Helios' Dark Love
**Lilac Dreams**
    Lord Helios' True Love

Scott Delaney

**Forward**

Cigarettes and Rocket Ships

Scott Delaney

**Pen to Paper**

What do I write
to the one whom I write,
one whom I see
when I pen new paper,
one giving ink
to vulnerable strokes,
one who believes
unlike others.

What do I etch,
when they get what I say,
without ever saying a word.

Cigarettes and Rocket Ships

Scott Delaney

**Lost**

Cigarettes and Rocket Ships

## Lineage

Without rowing -
without knowing,
sweet tranquil sound
rocking boat,
evoking bliss -
Helios.

Before he knows,
he knows the sea,
hidden secrets,
mysteries,
coastline ragged -
his to see.

Much more awaits,
much more to go.
Where he can be,
his to know.
This lineage -
his to grow.

## Amongst the Waves

Cautious lips,
azure eyes -
hungry hips
sway to sound,
wantonly.

Choc'late hair,
prideful neck -
shoulders bare
framing weight,
weightlessly.

Fearful tryst,
damaged past –
cautious bliss
sneaks a kiss,
longingly.

Another night soaked in hope;
chasing oneness, once again.

## Demigod Breath

Breath is life,
keeping me alive.
In. Out. In.
I am here, within.

Forty years,
broken dimensions.
In. Out. In.
With just compressions.

Filling lungs,
no hesitation.
In. Out. In.
Wants reparation.

Demigod
provides me purpose.
Simple touch…
In. Out. In - *Out. In.*

Now alive.
Now breathing.

## The Dopest of Dope

Coupling is troubling,
that's not the problem.
Trouble is troubling -
I can't be alone.

The need to connect -
empathize, realize,
self is not lonely
my self is alone.

One's hope can be found -
one's half can be whole.
That is the mission -
the dopest of dope.

Scott Delaney

**Shipwrecked**

Body shattered on the shore,
my heart buried under whores,
my self lost to all I had.
Shadowed me crawls from the sea.

Shin bone snapped in twenty-two,
eyelid ripping straight clean through,
mangled hand in coral rocks.
Ocean spray laps blood away.

Cold dark waters of past years,
erode essence into fear,
disembowel inner being.
Flailing self, Amongst the Waves.

Leukothea from the deep,
ethereal under me,
lifts me from the chill of surf.
Cradled chest, so caringly.

Envelops essence selflessly,
her glow washes over me,
calling sleep yet to come.
Finally, my heart is warm.

## The Myth

Leukothea stands in mist,
grounded on the pebbled shore,
watching sailors pass through dark,
search of safety, search of light.

The ocean her devotion,
those distressed in chopping waves.
Mother's instinct, wayward souls,
those as lost as she and me.

Sea salt air, soft yellow hair,
sinewy wrists, bend and twist,
brow smooth like midnight water,
resolute, watching over.

Ancient miles behind that smile,
greenstone eyes that save demise,
shipwrecked sailors lost at sea,
rescued many, now found me.

Scott Delaney

**Once**

Lost in the breast of another
who's tried to lose me, yet again.

Found by one who knows me now
and still my love cannot yet stand.

I try. I want. I try to bend.
Just to have it once. Again.

## Sun Blister

Long white casing suns
in simmering heat,
sea hag chains binding,
eating chiseled bone.
Fat seagulls pick, pluck
seeds from star-shrunk eyes,
chewing empty loins;
ravishing supple meat.

Humbled Helios,
adrift untethered-
dragged through shallow shoals,
succumbs, relentless
yellow-legged feasting,
snapping rotted bones.
Sea monsters devour
tragic, misled souls.

Assumed asylum
consumed my freedom,
leaving me bobbing
in tepid ocean.
I flee Leukothea;
safety of water,
first trekking inland
search for another.

Scott Delaney

**Lost-Found**

Cigarettes and Rocket Ships

## Empty Mind

I don't mind
an empty mind.
I don't get
a lot of rest.
My head spins
on rapid go;
thinking whirrs,
unyielding noise -
manic throes,
relentless thoughts;
half-knot wants,
forever haunts.

But today,
my head is calm.
Sun-filled wind -
renewed brain balm.
Won't last long.
It never does.
But for now,
it's epic peace -
next one brings
eternal ease.

## Warrior Fairy

Zim, bold King of Fairies -
chief illustrator
of wayward childhood;
lead interpreter
of dreams yet to be,
sleeping sleepless nights,
dancing longingly
with Kohol, Nico,
in dry summer heat.

Eyes, mischievous -
deft instigator
of grey temptations;
manipulator
of pursuant fears
welcoming sailor,
honored Helios
bringing storied tales
across angry sea.

Zim, boldfaced survivor -
escaped abuser
of dismantled homes,
willful resistor
of pain for today,
works to remember,
the love of lost loves,
of those departed –
his inspiration.

## Get By

Zim gets by somehow, someway,
has to muscle through this day,
morrow just too far away;
yesterday, too close for him.

Blackened ugly, haunting past
of lost days that always last;
brutal bedtimes forging masks,
terror realized, bathed in sin.

King Fairy can't yet repent,
mother ghosts will not relent,
Kohol made him confident;
barbaric times made him Zim.

## Picture Frames

Zim pictures himself in a picture frame,
his life zombies pressed queerly against glass,
squirming like earthworms on rain-wet sidewalk,
boiling in the sticky, sulfurous sun.

Monster fingers curl around outer edge,
muted alien voices clamoring,
screaming like he does, haunting all he was -
late daylight leaves him sleeping, while awake.

Nevermore flies in, taps relentlessly
on glass, riling up zombies of vile past -
safely squared away, hidden from the day,
not uncovered until he's lost his way.

"I don't know why I called you, Fairy King.
"I just called you, because I don't know why,"
squawks Raven, tap tap tapping much too fast
"I have arrived here somehow in your past."

Raven Nevermore will forever more
remind him of what's left, but those zombies
are captured, safely stored in pictured glass,
in a way that makes him feel… in control.

Zim is strong, not withdrawn, he'll bang that gong
until they're gone or well beyond the fringe.
He'll be left with amazing picture frames
framing everything of them - not him.

Scott Delaney

## The Challenge

When I was lost
Amongst the Waves
Zim prayed to pay
and free the knave.

When I was found,
I lost my head,
Zim set me free,
unburdened me.

We shared stories
tempted Kohol,
danced with Nico –
established "we".

Kohol's wanting,
proved too haunting,
she arranged to
put Zim to sleep.

Now each Sunday
I count to three,
pray tears hydrate
this dreaming thief.

My lifelong friend.
has no relief,
it is his grief,
that stole the free.

I hope to see him
one more day,
some other way -
just not this way.

## Eire Assassin

Boom! Ea is in the room,
tossing fistfuls of laughter;
like magical throwing stars -
each splits sides, effortlessly.

Eyes of mirth that bob and smirk,
takes piss like I wish I could,
karate chop that drops knees -
she wields "belly snort disease".

When she's done they're all well done -
bodies scattered, bent at waist,
sucking airdrops, taking gasps,
pleading hopeful for an end.

Eire Assassin, has struck again.

Scott Delaney

**Tug**

Slight tug,
on cusp of shirt,
not wanting to be put to sleep.
Body fighting deep,
awakening the weakness
of never wanting
to be alone.

## Cigarettes and Rocket Ships

We three tackle bourbon air,
Malibu skies, Miller dunes,
just to be – to truly be,
bonded alone, together.

Ardent friends defy space-time
within confines of our minds.
Outer space – adventure place,
choirs thoughts of smiles and pain.

Cigarettes and rocket ships –
incense masking all our trips.
We explore five days, four nights -
sage relief of well-earned strife.

Holding tight, with all our might,
we grip star-punched inner light,
true friends in this soulful way,
we find safety in today.

Scott Delaney

**Here**

Can't see, can't touch,
but know as much.
We aren't apart
or alone, so much -

you are always near.

Cigarettes and Rocket Ships

Scott Delaney

# Found

Cigarettes and Rocket Ships

## Nico

Jet-black hair, pale white skin
hung over well-worn bar.
Ruby lips like Garbo,
sipping rocky water,
slipping in and out of
empty conversation.

A red-bearded poet
croons last night's accolades
to captive audience.
(They're trying to rally -
happy hour is just
a few hours away.)

"*This* is what I'm wearing,
it was in your bedroom"
she says to bearded man
serenading barkeep
for one more martini.
"Definitely straight up."

Nico joins Helios,
sings wildly to power
of Grey Goose on the rocks,
pearled perfection embossed,
rising her – urging her,
from the doldrums of loss.

How it ends is how it begins -
one more good time, just one more time.

## Whispers

Effervescence
awakens me
from yesterday.

Softly whispering
happiness in
curious ears.

I now can catch
tomorrow in
pieces of today.

## Tried

I lied. (Or tried.)
fervent honest
dishonesty,
the bold-faced why's
of why I lived
the way I lied.

Manipulated.
(Or tried.) The lives
of family,
friends, partners, and
anyone else
to meet my ends.

Now, I confess.
Eat all my pain.
Share vanity;
error-filled ways.
How I am lost,
it is my way.

All I can do,
is simply be.
See if we'll live,
swap retold tales,
or hear stories
of new-found me.

I try. But it's
not up to me.

## Leper Hugs (Truth of Nico)

Our empty lust is lost
in eyes like charcoal dust,
sheathed in midnight morning.
Black-haired Nico, hustles.

Hollow words spill over,
never ending - seeing,
in eyes like empty thoughts,
engulfed by tired days.

Morning embrace hurried,
holding me in eyes like
leper hugs – vacuous,
with cold unwanted ways.

The warmth I felt
was boiled meat.

Scott Delaney

**Editing Insight**

Just realized I loved Nico then.
Completely as I could, back when.

Amongst the Waves. Leukothea.
Like every love I've felt since ten.

Like this feeling has always been,
like it will never be, again.

Those loves are lost, I can't pretend;
cannot begin to make amends.

**Fail Great**

Size of reward equates
to equitable risk.
If you haven't failed great,
enough hasn't been risked.

Scott Delaney

## Lilac Dreams

Fresh lilac dreams on mountain snow,
illuminate in winter calm,
trudging lightly, holding fiercely
to blanket hearth; warming wonder.

Mogul fields melt, launch us forward
toward frozen jump rocketing us
outside of space, defying Earth,
freeing us from this empty place.

Now that we are - now we explore
the breath of flight - freedom of light,
we may never come back to Earth.
I never knew I could, 'til leaning back to go.

## Defined

More than I could - should, ever find,
begging for hope, mends over time.

Breathe every breath; rest quiet mind,
in search of calm peace without try.

Truth, query, answer.
Our love is defined.

Scott Delaney

**All I've Found**

Scared to talk,
walk the walk,
hold, be held,
trust a lot.

Scared to cry -
hopeless try,
captured ease
then know why.

That is what I want.
All I've found, is more.

**Time Travelers**

We two are time travelers
exploring outer edges -
the vulnerabilities,
sustainable memories,
culpabilities of space.

Space - that place, outside the race
breathing deeply, sincerely,
as we rise into ether,
lose breath finding eagerness
in the odyssey of us.

Sun ascends in blink of eye,
the depth of your sighs, hard won
laugh lines that belie beauty
in your sighs, craves the sweetness
in our ours, no truthful lies.

Traveling through bound'ries of space,
traveling through unbounded time,
with the essence I'm knowing…
with the safety I'm meant to…
the one I've come here to find.

We are time travelers,
just starting our time.

Scott Delaney

# Epilogue

Cigarettes and Rocket Ships

Scott Delaney

**Truth**

Beauty to me
is resolute -
to have safety,
as truth.

Comfort to be,
at peace with Who -
know exactly,
no proof.

Tranquility,
all the way through -
it's what found me.
With you.

www.ingramcontent.com/pod-product-compliance
Lightning Source LLC
Chambersburg PA
CBHW051350040426
42453CB00007B/505